WHAT LEAVES MAY KNOW

Also by Paul Berry:

The Cries of Ashes (Scree, 1979)
Legacies (Scree, 1981)
Earth Musk and Country Dark (Outposts, 1982)
A Bequest of Fire (Outposts, 1985)
Homages and Holiday Snaps (Envoi, 1989)
Towards Babingley (Matador, 2023)

Social History:

Airfield Heyday (Jim Baldwin, 1989)

WHAT LEAVES MAY KNOW

Paul Berry

First published 2019
This edition 2024

Copyright © Paul Berry 2024

The moral right of the author has been asserted.

Apart from any fair dealing for the purposes of research or private study, or criticism or review, as permitted under the Copyright, Designs and Patents Act 1988, this publication may only be reproduced, stored or transmitted, in any form or by any means, with the prior permission in writing of the publishers, or in the case of reprographic reproduction in accordance with the terms of licences issued by the Copyright Licensing Agency. Enquiries concerning reproduction outside those terms should be sent to the publishers.

Troubador Publishing Ltd
Unit E2 Airfield Business Park,
Harrison Road, Market Harborough,
Leicestershire LE16 7UL
Tel: 0116 279 2299
Email: books@troubador.co.uk
Web: www.troubador.co.uk

ISBN 9781805144663

British Library Cataloguing in Publication Data.
A catalogue record for this book is available from the British Library.

Printed by Printed and bound by CPI Group (UK) Ltd, Croydon, CR0 4YY
Typeset in 10pt Minion Pro by Troubador Publishing Ltd, Leicester, UK

For Tina
for believing, encouraging
and simply being there still

ACKNOWLEDGEMENTS

What Leaves May Know was first published in 2019 in a limited issue by Colin Blundell at Hub Editions. Sadly, Colin passed away as this revision was being prepared. I treasure memories of visits to the house, crammed with books and artworks, where he lived with Janet, along the banks of the Nene in Wingland on the Norfolk/Lincolnshire border. I am fortunate to have benefited from his time and boundless creative energy, generously given as an editor and publisher, but, above all, from the friendship, wisdom and encouragement of an inspirational poet and teacher.

This new edition includes six additional poems. Grandmother in Winter was first collected in *Earth Musk and Country Dark* (Outposts, 1982); while You, A Pilgrim Perhaps, To A Roman Wall Auxiliary, Through an English Middle March, Drytime Traveller and Notes on Returning appeared in *A Bequest of Fire* (Outposts, 1985).

Acknowledgement is made to editors of the following magazines who first published poems collected here: *Iota, Sepia, Breathe, Bogg, Pirate Bogg, Boggers All* (USA), *Links, Positively Poetry, Dial 174, The People's Poetry, Poetry Now, Start, Speakeasy, Moorland Review, Ore* and *Envoi*.

Thanks are due to the editors and compilers of anthologies who previously included some of the poems which follow: *The Best of Poetry Now, Envoi 1991 Anthology, Second Time Single, Treasured Times, A New Dawn, Through All the Length of Days, The*

Gregory Poems 1983-84, *Emotional Ties* and *Poet's England*. Poems selected as finalists in the Sandburg Livesay Award were published in America in award anthologies for 1997, 1998, 2000 and 2004 by UnMon Press, Pittsburgh.

At Troubador Publishing I am pleased to acknowledge the inputs of Chloe May, Jonathan White, Andrea Johnson and, significantly, Jessica Woodward. Enthusiastically and with commendable attention to detail, Jess project-managed the transformation of a slide-bindered stack of typed sheets into this perfect bound paperback, graced once again by the creative skill and vision of cover designer Chelsea Taylor. And Jeremy Thompson helped ensure fewer errors have claimed squatter's rights among the ensuing pages.

I remain grateful to Sue Burge and the late Colin Blundell for providing writing workshop inputs where some of these poems had their beginnings. Special thanks go to Adrian Eden and Anna Pugh, at By the Book in Hunstanton, for their enthusiasm and practical support.

Yet once again, it is Tina who merits the deepest appreciation, not only for suggesting the additional poems for this collection but, most especially, for helping create and share in many of those wonderful, significant moments that oft-times find their way into poems.

CONTENTS

Grandmother in Winter	1
Calendar 1988	3
Watching Winter	4
Moving On	5
A Certain Shrine	7
Journey Home	9
Whistling Tree	11
Cutting Corners	12
On a High Hill	14
For My Father, Flyer	16
Teddy, Wiggs and Ned	17
You, a Pilgrim, Perhaps	19
What Leaves May Know	20
Last Bus	22
Sneaking Back	23
Clwyd Again	25
West Princes Street Gardens	26
Family Get-Together	27
Guarding	28
Lessons	29
Wait, Moments	30
Big Boys & Bannisters	31
First Day at School	33
Towards Freedom	35
At Norwich Cathedral	36
Wootton Marshes	37

Cycling to Sandringham	38
Of Stars and Sand	40
Coming of Age	41
Valentine from Wendy	42
Brandeston School Oak	43
Visit After a Death	44
City Crematorium	46
Far Countries	47
Old Year's Eve, Wells	49
Twelfth Night	50
Remembering on GNER	51
Union Farm	52
Through an English Middle March	54
i) Redesdale	54
ii) Carter Bar	55
iii) Dinner at Otterburn	56
To a Roman Wall Auxiliary	57
A Prospect of Durham	59
Llanberis Pass	60
June on Snow Hill	61
Shore	62
On a Stratford Street	64
Discovering Dad	66
And What of Ploughmen?	68
Night Noises	70
Looking at Remains	71
Drytime Traveller	75
Notes on Returning	77
Papworth Poems	78
i) Some women enter your heart...	78
ii) Veering	79

> If poetry comes not as naturally as leaves to a tree,
> it had better not come at all.
>
> From a letter to John Taylor, February 27, 1818
> **John Keats**
> (1795-1821)

> Love! Love! When we wandered here together,
> Hand in hand! Hand in hand through the sparkling weather,
> From the heights and hollows of fern and heather.
>
> God surely loved us a little then.
>
> From *The Swimmer*
> **Adam Lindsay Gordon**
> (1833-1870)

GRANDMOTHER IN WINTER

Between your children's visits
and news of places and ways
distant and still wonderful to you,
there is time to tally pails of pebbles,
or recall juices blacking your young hands
and a scent of earth, growing things and toil
so broth thick the air tasted of it.
Fields have no more need of you now
and mouths you worked to feed
make different demands.
Time sees to that too.

Time to watch steam curling from pans
simmering among coals cradling them.
You have watched the ashes cling; a few at first
but now pan-caked and crusted, wanting renewal.
(The fire has that effect but needing heat
these days there is nowhere else to sit.)
When cooking is done, sticks are burned:
thornbull and nutwood cracking the hours
toward evening, shooting occasional
incendiaries to fade and die unseen,
far from the business of burning.

Between watching waterfalls of melting snow
and making plans to visit the village again,
there is time to smile down the years,
when cake and the slow tick of minutes
were seldom seen or heard. But no hurry today:
sit back and watch flames eat tissue
from the gift a grandchild brought.
Now, when work is done, there is
time like there never was before.

CALENDAR 1988

This is the gift of years:
figures which regaled bargains,
the price of tea and cauliflowers,
marshal birthdays from memory
and with totals in the eighties
find uncertain refuge in words:
'They say I do well for my age',
never knowing or hearing who did.

This is the gift of years:
buses go unhailed, cupboards empty
and pennies holiday in secret places.
Market day trips are less regular
and in the shelter friends enquire
of your health and whereabouts
in the weekly wait-for-the-bus
review of village uncertainties.

This is the gift of years:
twelve pages with pretty scenes
chosen to brighten days lined up
by the week on a printed grid.
Inked numbers and mottoes
tease with their promises of time,
belie the weight of spent years
keeping you pinned to a chair.

WATCHING WINTER

Swiss roll, a slice of Sunday's chicken;
then after breakfast, other rituals –
reading the parish letter, early Christmas cards,
hearing who caught Thursday's market bus,
sat where, said what, their absorbing buys.
Or a sortie to the larder-cold front room
retrieving chilled treasures only seen on stalls.
Then resting easy, spirits beyond speaking before
goodbyes, give-my-love and remember-me-to's.

No reason to spoil or sully fireside peace,
chiselled and worn by slow Smith's ticks.
Sparks starred a fire-stone's sooty heaven,
coals nestled clinker-crusted cooking pans,
coffeed milk heaved to the flame's bidding.
From hissing flares of forests millennia ago,
the scorching roasting glow of burning
speckled legs of watching idlers resting souls,
warming a dim kitchen's frugal sixty watts.

Sometimes at wintertide her eyes were watery,
I thought from the heat and envied her this idyll.
She has gone now and down beet-dirtied roads
December days are short and squeezed of light.
I recall her alone, craning to spot a neighbour,
a glimpse, some movement in drizzled emptiness,
beyond windows pinned with Christmas wrap
that coloured leaden winter and blotted damp,
though never her tears shed silently for spring.

MOVING ON

Eighty three and nearer heaven
she casts off, one November day,
her cottage, like a discarded skin
whose season is done and goes
by way of ward and walking frame
into state assisted closing time.

Now water comes warm from taps,
heat comes easy on every side
and Parker Knolls support brittle
posture correct Edwardians
suspicious of life's luxuries,
the unbidden arrival of food.

Strange the home a husband bought
which once met their every need,
should in later widowed days
demand more from her than age
or precious energy could give.
And she no stranger to labour,

clearing half a field of stones,
unable now to bear a pail of coal
or kneel low at the grate to clear
the dust of each day's vital burning,
or carry without shaking,
kettles of water from the flames.

We understand more clearly now
her months of not giving in,
clinging, refusing to admit defeat:
the mantel shelf becoming dustier,
the whole house needing heat,
a larder stocked with cold cooked meat.

Wide spread curtains and doors ajar
no longer welcome prized daylight:
today it comes in fluorescent tubes
anytime and one payment covers all,
avoiding the quarterly consternation
of a light bulb's awful extravagance.

Sit back, enjoy the emptied days,
manicures, morning tea and fuss
of people paid to carry and care
as you did once, earning, eking out
your father's money catching moles
with a serving girl's shillings.

Relax: you have earned this rest.
But do not forget kitchen ewers
holding well-water cold as crystal
and the hearth-side's holy light
drawing all your children back.
No regrets, no wish to return.

But it is not the scent of ageing
drawing tears, forcing silent smiles,
on the faces of sons and daughters
with nowhere to come back to,
nowhere to call home, now lodestones,
so easily millstones, are abandoned.

A CERTAIN SHRINE

She has made her peace,
settled affairs and gone now,
left the place of flint and clunch
her husband laboured hard for.
Half her life she lived alone
without a mate, in his nest;
his legacy to feed and clothe
sending her to strawberry fields
or bringing fowl to the hearth
to pluck and dress for dinners.

Later the state gave money,
her children fruit and flowers
and she shared her fireside
with any who cared to call.
There dawn's stillness broke,
quietly blurring towards day.
Callers strained to hear above
the flames' tormented teasing
of spilling, hissing milk pans,
the potatoes bubbling to mash.

No more sugared shortcakes
from the flour-dusted early hours
of fond remembered baking days.
Breakfast for her postman's rest,
bringing news of nearby towns,
blueys from a daughter GI bride
and, once, a fire grate from Holt.
Or the insurance man's premium:
pastries, paybook and coins laid
meticulous on the table's chenille.

Now the cottage stands empty,
chimneys tumbled, garden wild
and in a district famed for shrines
there hangs a peace in dereliction,
a quiet deeper than before.
After she left the message wires
to Binham and beyond were buried,
north winds no longer lamenting
the news and notes of birds
at rest on the telegraph staves.

JOURNEY HOME

Four harvests ago, yes so few,
Thursdays in the small market town
closed this way, along this road;
leaving behind her tiny shops
(electric, sweet and Topping Stores,
Butcher Broady trussed and dressed),
the blesséd stall-lined pavements
barbed, tangled with thorns of people.

Now in some other year
on a Thursday, the day and time,
she leaves the same town
and the cosy council home
she was lately transplanted in.
Having green fingers she knew
of cuttings and difficulties
taking root in new places.

Once laden with groceries,
veg when gardening ceased
or thick socks for a neighbour
who seldom cycled abroad.
Today flowers weigh her down.
The dark limousine meanders
slow as a market day bus
only bigger, cleaner windows.

And so she journeyed home
past farm, knoll and old familiars
joining the route once walked
for pension, bingo, fetes and friends,
Sunshine Bread and nice sliced ham.
And while away newcomers came
closing, converting Post Office Stores.
Only the church keeps open doors

to welcome the old returning.
Four it took to help her out;
no shopping trolley to lift,
no stick for stabbing puddles.
And for the first time in a life
of Thursdays home from town,
no clutch of toffees and mints
for the driver being on time.

WHISTLING TREE

There is a gap on the sky
where Whistling Tree was,
a field littered by twigs
and piles the woodsman left
finishing the storm's work.
And when there is nothing,
no sign to remind what stood,
how long before memories mist,
fade, or even hearts forget?

Already ivy creeps, advancing,
covering the jagged stump,
the corner adapting to days
without its century sentinel.
Whole lifetimes it had served,
offering shelter, marking midpoint
between one village and the next:
permanent, familiar, welcoming,
growing old without our knowing.

Somewhere is a monochrome print:
a small boy staying with his gran
picnicking against a grassy bank
shaded by a just discernible trunk.
Now a splinter saved from the sawyer
is shared, shown to sons later on,
reminding once there stood a tree,
and the hands holding this relic,
warming memories, were once a child's.

CUTTING CORNERS

Their first time home
in black and white.
Years it took,
a mutual's alchemy
turning jugged sixpences
into a '50s assemblage
of finest Fletton bricks:
a nest fit for a clerk's boy.

Pictured on the path
the nestling, fledging –
his back to the bungalow,
with metal framed windows
which wept in winter
and the coal bunker
which became lookout,
car and covered wagon.

Ahead, the shed,
tongued and grooved,
where bikes and benches
cooked in creosoted dark.
And then the fence,
the passing trains to Wells,
Monday's drying managed
around the mixed good's smuts.

Cleaner, frequent DMU's obliged,
grinding ballast to gunpowder
while he hid from any crash.
And talk of destroying –
this same boy, a pedal car,
metal hubs and ill-judged steering
scuffing corners, chipping bricks,
slowly demolishing the dream.

ON A HIGH HILL

Is it concern for my son
who, slipping on scree,
might fall, bruising like a peach,
or leaning into the valley
overbalance the peak
making his triumphal wave
to family shadowed far below?

Or is it concern for me,
selecting footfalls with care
thinking I do for two,
begging him beware the edge
where my eyes and ears
will not connect for balance?
He commands the hill, he dares.

Closing eyes, I sway,
see this mound years ago:
a day trip with my father
leaning for frequent hand holds,
dragging breathlessly behind,
who fought, flew against nations
but now is fazed by heights.

Does daring fade inverse to age
'til fear builds high as a hill
which an adult and father
will cover with bravado
thin as grass on rocky crags,
which falling, slipping feet
just as easily expose.

Thorpe Cloud, Derbyshire

FOR MY FATHER, FLYER

It is not too late for thanks
discovering among stats and facts
of every one hundred who flew to
dare dark and our neighbours now,
just twenty-four survived, unharmed.
Figures become sons, become fathers,
and I, heir to one of another few,
grateful to luck and forgotten crews
and Queens of the Skies, he said once
of the old black behemoths he knew.

His son at twenty was a college boy,
swapping bombs for books in cosy billets,
daring perhaps to miss a lecture or two.
Then the son becomes a parent, reassesses
approaching forty, his father thirty more.
Beyond clouds again an old enemy waits,
stacking odds with each passing year.
Today we cannot trust or chance to luck,
and it is never too late for thanks
these days when tours are nearly up.

TEDDY, WIGGS AND NED

After decades of camphoric dark,
wardrobed, secreted away and lost,
they are united, together again:
the straw dog with worn out fur,
Ned the horse with blue glass eyes
and him, their master still.

Time was when they were four
and they, his cuddled cosies,
lay content when beds were trains
while he, demented divan driver,
dieseled, diddly-dee and dumming
through night's dark tunnels.

Yet the bear who travelled then
now lives in some distant place,
crack pad pawed and growl-less,
a gift of love as though to show
the girl who shared new pillow talk
the child she came too late to know.

Today for forgotten childhood's sake
his wife brings the two to bed again,
they who cushioned befuddled falls
from train to track, bed to floor,
the guardians of close-eyed dreams
when one slow day became the next.

Yet this night they bring no succour,
stirring him from sleep, their firmness
leaving impressions deep and numbing.
He lifts them out, hugs another shape:
the scent and touch of skin not straw,
those comforts he traded a teddy for.

YOU, A PILGRIM, PERHAPS
(*Walsingham*)

Our wanderings never brought us to this place:
the eagerness to love forbade tarrying here.
Only now, less urgent, can some newer wisdom
understand these lessons from the stones.

For it is not merely the majesty of ruin,
doorways to nowhere remaindered among daffodils
or east windows breaking the garden's gaptoothed smile.

Former glories would be sad, faded thus,
but for pilgrims who know the worth of these remains.

Hearts have their ruins, when love,
built with hope enough, crumbles.

And if, during an absence of some other he,
or a suddenly heard song that held us once,
you become a pilgrim wandering through

remains of dreams we built, and hearing again
echoes from those yesterdays, you recall
visions we tried hard, through sighs,
to find, and remembering primal urgings

smile that time we spent was not in vain,
the rubble of our hasty building affirming
a faith in hands that seek your secrets now,
then I can value the ruins that are left.

WHAT LEAVES MAY KNOW

Once
   girls unknown
   infatuation fresh
   romance untried

        this leaf knew
        spring
        & maybe him

        young, easy on hills
        lithe between trees
        piggy-backing girls

        no, a chosen one
        all summer long
        and ever after

        lacking the Amen

Now
   30 leaf-falls later
   100 miles from
   arboreal city parks

        years divide
        amass, outweigh
        they make mulch

        & some survive
        sun bleached
        skeletal, dry

        a treasured leaf
        by his bedside
        where she sleeps

        if only in dreams

LAST BUS

Along the summered routes of memory
two people go. An evening empty coach
of comfortable corporate moquette

seats where she lay, head on his lap,
lost beyond finding or words, in worlds
new found this night by them alone –

denied all others (save drivers glancing up,
in mirrors reminded of their former loves
and how fast untimetabled time passes).

Among dancing seats through dusky shires
to terminals in nonsleeping electric cities.
Then chill beery streets to Broad Marsh buses:

likely a crowded local, stopping every stop
for air to freshen the warm tobacco fug,
seeding suburban streets with happy inebriates.

Amid onboard banter, low busts and bellies,
his arm round her slight shoulder, shielding
against the coarse intimacy of last buses home.

SNEAKING BACK

Like two pert breasts locals said
of mounds of motorway waste,
grassed now and part of the Moor
they cycled over on the one red
rusting Raleigh of her childhood.
A dip, grazed by freeman's cows,
like a navel, the path taken now
a barely visible caesarean scar.

Here faltering lights, a creaking gate,
the road to neat, trim estates where
one time merchantmen bought bricks
to house their sweetest daughters.
They allowed boyfriends camp beds,
anchor-blanketed for northern nights,
gave flasks from their wholesale firms
for coffee on the long day coach home.

Years have not changed the house,
the imprint of a generation stays;
beyond grey nets her parents shuffle
among galleries of grandchildren.
And what if she should visit now,
maybe call with lobelia for setting out?
Would he hurry past, or watch away,
safe by their letters' posting box?

Or walk up and say... what exactly?
After thirty years of heat and cold
the Thermos had to be replaced?
Recall times lang syne to bridge years
and risk events pushing them apart?
Or, not daring to sully memory's gloss,
departing by suddenly familiar ways?
A last look at idle shipyard cranes

beckoning like slow mantises once,
the blues and twos in Spital Tongues,
the city clamouring beyond the Moor.
Leaving, remembering sights, sounds
and passions time has barely changed.
Here they stopped at a rare bench,
cuddled, their laps cradling secrets,
eyes ever on pert hills close to hand.

CLWYD AGAIN

Most days they walked each way,
the route from Halkyn mountain
to holy wells and sea level civilisation
where bus routes began and ended,
twenty forgotten summers ago.
Each too much the other's to know,
or care, of the distances covered
to the cottage at Pen Ucha'r Plwyf
where, behind 1930's coloured glass
August called, slate cold and dark.

Now with ease, comfort and wheels
he revisits with wife and children
searching heathered hills for wreckage,
the places of old love's dying days,
but there is nothing to see or salvage.
A dial on a dashboard turns eight,
reminding how passion lean and young
held out, un-noticed at the time,
against the sun and tar blistered roads,
the long and shimmering empty miles.

WEST PRINCES STREET GARDENS

Unaware of trains waiting on Waverley
or crowds along Princes Street,
two lovers in a public park
where worlds have their beginning,
orbit and every function
in an embrace, a word or look.
Futures are for planning together
though the beds in different towns.

Unaware down the years someone
browsing the all night bookshop,
will hear among the remaindered piles
a quiet background of forgotten songs,
arcing recollection of this same place,
recalling gardens, grass and love.

Unaware they will return, searching,
fixing castle, paths and trees
to find where, one spring of memory,
promises were made and passions begun.
Familiar views are rediscovered
yet mere looking cannot find the place.
With weeds the grass seems coarser.
Where, how did they lay so long?

And if the lovers knew it would be so,
one could predict, perhaps, chagrin
that someone makes their shrine a grave.
Moist-eyed disbelief would follow next,
hardly recognising it is one of them
and they have returned, alone.

FAMILY GET-TOGETHER

Now at last we hold him,
though hours are nothing now.
He gazes with new blue eyes:
the justification for an assembly
with songs for leaving, speeches,
flowers, tears and meringues.
Now we hold the kick inside,
the rapid heartbeat on a screen,
the hard to discern shape,
thumb sucking even then.
Here, the answers we waited for,
yet how he looks or like who
scarcely matter now we know.
And questions for years to come
are too vague to worry over now.
Mums and dads, a phone call away
vesting them grandma and grandpa,
will tease us with mum and dad.
Now at last we hold him.
Empty wards fade from view as we,
visibly a first time family,
swaddled in love, proud, relieved,
aching, tired, cuddle close,
locked, held in each other's wonder.

GUARDING

Total surrender. Sleep is yours:
it is the milky haze of light, air
and an untroubled library hush
we have long forgotten.
My part in this, beyond remembering,
is guarding your peace,
keeping dark worlds at bay.
With moistened finger
I dab away a harvest midge,
too curious, too close.
It should always be now:
trading security for smiles,
keeping you as cotton-tight safe
as I imagine my father did me.

And did he know that moment
as faces fold into frowns,
eyelids flicker, lips purse
and soft skin-downs stretch
when dreams tease and taunt?
And I, as impotent as he,
will never summon means enough
to do what my blood screams
I do for this sweetest blood of mine.
What did they do, our fathers,
with little more than fingers
freshly licked and the only arms
the holding, enfolding kind,
to keep encroaching cares away?

LESSONS

On the day you offered biscuit
I bowed at fisted Rich Tea half moons
to break off my crumbs and eat.
You smiled at our first sharing.
On the day you offered Marmite
I bent to your finger's pincer grip,
breaking, taking bread and eating.
You laughed that you should feed me.

On the day you offered book
I did not move towards your gift,
a tempting morsel of saliva'd card pulp
eight teeth chewed from *Spot at the Fair*.
You waited for something to happen,
but nothing, only reasons you couldn't know.
First your outstretched arm fell,
your legs bent, giving way to sitting,
then tears from some dark well
broke across your perfect face.
Strange a body in a squirrel suit
could crumple, sob and suffer so.

Thus the first unwitting hurt was done,
the age old bruising of father and son.
When years have heaped misunderstandings
and the balance of wisdom, or of right,
rests level between us, or is tipped,
I may remember again that lesson:
when innocent offers of love are spurned,
the pain and the impossibility of amends.

WAIT, MOMENTS

During the first-word weeks
there was a typical day
balancing plates, demands
and two tiny, determined hands
tugging at trousers, hems,
urging us to stop and play.
We suggested: "Wait a moment."

Then in the parroting period
we requested he prepare for bed;
unconcerned he played on
with Danish bricks, trains and
hearing us now making demands,
nonchalantly turned and said
distinctly: "Wade a mummet."

And for him it probably seemed
moments were for wading through,
long hours, whole days to be endured,
impeding progress to each new stage;
while we would have the moments wait,
prolonging innocence until the last
and stall the headlong rush of age.

BIG BOYS & BANNISTERS

On the seventh night of Christmas
an old year marshals for departure
and doors are opened and closed,
to distant ships' hooters and jeering
welcoming in a newer, fresher year.
He lays unperturbed, undisturbed
by ritual or celebration, untouched
by petty concern with passing time.

Knees close to chest, he kneels
cocooned by covers in a shape
reminiscent of some recent place.
Chrysalis-like he emerges from sleep,
each day closer to the boy, the man.
Was it just three short years ago
he was measured in dividing cells
who now reaches half his adult height?

On the eighth day of Christmas
he will choose the warm swaddling
of his mother's arms but answer
when she asks who is her baby,
"Not me, I'm a big boy now."
His day and year begins sorting
teddies, toys and tickets, arms filled
for his sure-footed progress downstairs.

Just six of our short months before
stair gates guarded this descent
and we were sherpas who guided,
shadowing the ascent of tricky slopes
lined by his former babists and baninins.
Now he refuses proffered hands and help,
confidently descends alone. It is a big boy
who can say bannisters, and reach them.

FIRST DAY AT SCHOOL

In weather befitting
ending a family monopoly
of care and influence,
we brave early morning drizzle
and heavy, dull skies, sombre
for his first day at school.
In a state provided room
furnished for Lilliputians
we hand him over: neck-tied,
long-trousered like a baby man.
His school uniform is blue,
the shade of hospital blankets
just four birthdays ago.

Our departure is hasty,
calculated and bewildering
before white strip lights
betray our tears to him.
Yet he will cope with separation,
fifty unfamiliar friends or foes
and playtime's capering circus
with a strength and resolution
the older, wiser and wet-eyed envy.
At times we ached for peace,
but this empty silence cloys:
quiet dropping cold all round,
an emptiness needing filling.

Returning, reunited, his joy breaks
briefly into subconscious protest,
a mood registering resentment
at those who took him there
and will again tomorrow.
Tomorrow. How many days is that?
Later, tired by timetabled time,
exhausted by stories and sticking,
he cuddles a familiar bear in bed.
The pillow puckers his lip,
Bugs Bunny-like, as babies sleep,
and for the short night's passing
he is briefly given back.

TOWARDS FREEDOM

Six years have left their mark
on the bedroom height chart,
now worn by faint inked lines
chronicling each month's growth.
With sticky tape and paper
and abundant whimsicality
he fashions his own.
To inches he adds places,
drawn worlds to grow towards.
Completed he lays it out,
invites us down to the floor
to discover where we are.

After the first few feet, Freedom,
and he is almost there,
aspiring too quickly towards
mum in Noughts and Crosses Land.
I maintain a loftier view,
detached by sellotape,
hoping he enjoys the freedom
he will soon grow through
and games along the way.
Betimes he'll be a tall as dad
whose head already brushes
the crayoned clouds of Heaven.

AT NORWICH CATHEDRAL

In cathedral precincts we once broke bread,
spilled juice, set episcopal pigeons tug o'warring
on discarded crusts milk teeth could not shred.

Never expected a return nine summers later
when, robed and scapulared, a son would sing,
his sweet treble rising, taking its place

in lofty Norman heavens, vaulted and bossed.
We listened, proud of one among the many,
amazed how he moved from Steps to Stainer,

adding his simple offering to nine hundred years:
legacy of monks, masons and elaborate geometry;
monument to Caen stone and buttered bread.

WOOTTON MARSHES

Easy riding on the flat between neat fields
corrugated by new season's potatoes and CAT tracks,
iridescent with stick free peas, maybe mange tout.

No one comes here unless there is a job to do.
Even tractormen are few, the marsh unpeopled,
its lack of shelter or recreation unforgiving.

A job, or empty evening and birthday bike to try
beside die-straight dykes emptying at distant banks,
a place so new they still drain fluid from its lung.

There beyond tide-marks of flotsam leavings
are saltings, good for geese, Vinegar Middle
and Bulldog Sands, canine free but not pup.

On banks like barren tropic isles, seals bask
where broken-back coasters once rusted
breached by tides and careless reading of charts.

Inland a home village, huddling at the edge,
further away than before, still closer than later
while ditch, drain and pump create more polder.

Salt, vinegar, potatoes, peas and easily eastward
pedals flesh, meat: a father and son racing each other
and sudden skies that will soak both man and marsh.

CYCLING TO SANDRINGHAM

Cycling a trackbed to Sandringham:
rabbits, pheasants and peewits where
Tsars, prime ministers, crowned heads
and dead heads travelled to audiences,
entrained to palaces or State repose.

Soaked and silvered fields catch up sun.
We halt at a bridge Beeching's axe broke
over fast flowing waters where St Felix
came inland to build his church,
ivied now and ruined, a short row away.

Long shadows tease ghostly platelayers
in briared and brambled broken huts.
Pausing for breath I tell my son all this,
of others who passed this way
and footplates spilling shards of coal.

I recreate, enthuse, but barely eight
his cares and concerns are immediate:
chill westerlies dew his nose, impede.
No privy hedges on this watered land;
shelter and salvation not close to hand.

Greying to seed with a stock of years,
I savour pasts, they cloud and fog.
For him history is mere distraction,
a tiresome headwind hindering futures
where bathrooms and warmth await.

Note: The King's Lynn–Hunstanton branch line was not among closures proposed in Richard Beeching's report, The Reshaping of British Railways (1963), but services ended on May 5 1969.

OF STARS AND SAND

Here in a mother's hand, moments,
discoveries, quirks and kindnesses.
Each, like a star, marvelled at,
in isolation separate and wonderful;
easily lost among heaven's other lights.

First words, drawings, handshapes,
food, friends and those first kisses
each unforgettable yet forgotten
but for words to revive memory
from the sheer blitz of growing up.

With no intention to forget
we have done so, imperceptibly,
as instants have massed, layered
and like sands peppered their escape
however tightly held or prized.

Her alchemy turns time into words
for touching and sparking dull memory
and among the careful history
of him, for him and lives yet to be,
we remember fragments of our own.

COMING OF AGE

for Mollie

Tears were not always secret:
once they fell openly, with ease,
brought home by the faceful
with grazed knees and stings
to the nest your arms made
for a body's warm balm, kind words
and the healing of familiar scents.
There was a place for you then.

Today you came upon him
in a glazed and red-eyed emptiness
with no need of plasters or creams.
Adult games are cruel and cutting,
new pride and passions stay tender
and sons who snuggled for comfort
now need solitude to bear
the weight of tears men cry.

VALENTINE FROM WENDY

Sweet sentiments, rough across coarse
all-there-was-to-hand yellowed paper.
A heart, blood red beneath crayoned
rainbows hoping *Happy Valentim's day.*
Inside, the pencilled challenge almost
risen to: *for my teecher from Wendy.*
No need for anonymity when barely nine;
wait for sparks to die and backs to turn
on struggles with spelling and learning.

Finding her faded home-made envelope,
what would she say knowing it was kept
two decades, not among loft dusty piles
of letters from first love's old campaigns
but treasure-filled spare room drawers?
Her lank bobbed hair and scally smile
recollected, a child's innocent hope
a student teacher have a happy day,
that rarest commodity in Cotton End.

The day recalled was good as her wish.
But what of hers? Does she remember?
Him with cheap chalk from a college shop
and foolscap padded plans to elevate.
Did they raise her to peaceful suburbs,
those clean-aired hills he came from
with files brimming good intentions?
Did anything mark or touch her life
the way her simple thought did his?

BRANDESTON SCHOOL OAK

You are: a visit to gran's,
a favourite armchair, comfy, worn;
the best teacher in the world.

They bring me to visit,
introduce me. You say nothing.
Me: "They have told me much about you,

the safe arbour of your branches' reach
giving time, a space, a place
to reflect or slow passing days."

But does my wonder sound hollow –
too many winters fogging eyes
to see the god in a tree?

Or is that, beyond the river's turn,
wounded bark screams as sawteeth cut
and wood smoke taints the air.

We kill for a full grate,
maim for a table of English oak.
What then for our children,
their cares, or birds?

VISIT AFTER A DEATH

On the third day after death
I leave the office and daylight
for their open-handed welcome
to the shrine of their uncertainty,
cocooned by curtains against a world
where grieving should not spill.

It is as though, out too long,
she will return from shopping,
or some far-off other-where
and find everything the same:
her open bag in need of closing,
discarded when the doctor came.

Her lover, for he was so once,
takes the tea his daughter brews
in a mug of painted forget-me-nots,
For The World's Best Mum in pink
and three day's solace in tannin runs.
A wedding album close at hand.

His son grows bowed and pale
in the week's half-lit emptiness,
broken by fetching, with the dog,
papers with *Mother's Tragic Death*
for family and friends far away,
and his secret, most troubled heart.

Of all the three, he says the least,
showing his sugar paper card for mum,
words regretting past naughtiness,
telling of his love that went unsaid.
"Two socks lost in the wash already,"
dad reminds to stall their heavy tears,

"lost without trace, not even a pair."
Son gives the smile his parent needs,
recalls clean socks stacked each week,
ice-cream trifles, stories at tuck-in time,
and retreats to bedrooms with thick walls,
built against worlds where tomorrows wait.

CITY CREMATORIUM

Safe inside cars, her brothers and sisters
stay warm, nursing their fears and frailties,
warding off November and pneumonia.
Rarely together these days, they wait alone
dutifully, or park alongside remembering,
wondering who next, waiting on valedictions,

for her unfamiliar hymns to snare them.
An attentive undertaker with audio tape
compensates for the organist councils cut.
A bowlered DJ for midday crem-karaoke,
50 Deathly Favourites of Ease and Repose.
The unwary stumble, the cautious mime.

Outside a memorial water feature trickles
like the forgotten tap in her empty flat.
Starlings in mourning chatter and mimic
grief, the long farewells and leavings.
Solemn men rake neat piles of leaves
and discreet flames tidy an aunt away.

FAR COUNTRIES

Okra and kandalla
at the corner shop,
cooking oil drums
at your mother's door,
have numbed your lips,
dulled thoughts
and snuffed faint flames
from childhood days
which revisiting
should have fanned.
You walk streets
where fifty years ago
you ran, dilly-carted
or trammed all day for 6d,
seeking the reassurance
beginnings can bring
when endings loom near.
Worn Fords pass you.
Dark elders sit bewildered
behind shirt-sleeved sons,
lighter skinned, driving easy,
at home in streets that lose you.
You came to childhood places,
found Sanskrit, strangers
and I saw the child in you:
confused by a world
you thought you knew,
wondering where you'd been,
if it were ever here.
No one keeps the rights

to roots they grow from.
They are passed on, renewed
or lost forever. Ask others.
Ask greying men in Cortinas,
moist-eyed from wandering
the far countries of memory
where okra and kandalla grow.

OLD YEAR'S EVE, WELLS

Across dusk's fading margin
a tick of geese in hooting formation
marks the passing of December.

Quayside gift shops announce sales
but it's Blue Cross Day already
for seagulls squabbling over bins
and cold post-Christmas chips.

A dredger engine throbs lazily
while in his dieseled dark
its master regulates the beat,
oblivious to the day, sentiment,
hourglasses and passing time:
sand and shifting his livelihood.

Here years fade without ritual,
nothing marks beginning or end.
Only the harbourmaster's office
carries among warnings of tides,
red flags and imported mad dogs,
a chalked blackboard message:

Pse keep all berths CLEAR

suggesting possible replacement
by something bigger, better,
for an old and emptied year
quietly slipping moorings
and drifting, drifting away.

(1979)

TWELFTH NIGHT

Ritualistically, each eve of Epiphany,
we banish the tree outside, still new
though bare, dry and boney-branched
stripped of fairy bulbs and fripperies;
take down moulting tinselled fringes
sons sellotaped to bedroom shelves;
ease shirt pins from familiar holes,
that anchored Paul Jones garlands
or held the tissued bells we blew
to ring midwinter through.

Twelfth Night and clearing Christmas.
A month, a room and lives are tidied
lest winter finds us cosy, napping.
But silver strands and pine needles
defy small cyclones or mere suction,
and surface on carpets in summer.
Ancient finds, like forgotten relics
of tree worshipping, light-loving tribes
decking hearths and cribs with glitter
for a transient magic to ease dark days.

REMEMBERING ON GNER

After warnings a whistle starts them:
train journeys and troops over the top
and Great North Eastern's remembrance.
Piped shrill through carriage speakers,
silence, marshalled, comes to attention.
November's poppies parade on lapels,
or mastheads of Sun and Times.

Along the Flying Scotsman's route
bomber country's rain-glazed fields:
a season or troop movement away
from winter wheat or Flander's mud,
ruined runways and pillboxes pass,
skeletal trees guard headlands,
propane mortars defend seedbeds.

Enter a tunnel: remembrance spoils
for want of visual clues or popping ears.
Landscapes remind longer with traces,
signs men mark, then move away from.
Before Grantham the guard says time is up,
gives corporate thanks and reminds York
next stop, lest by remembering we forgot.

Note: GNER: Great North Eastern Railway who
provided train services on the East Coast Main
Line April 1996 to December 2007

UNION FARM

Cutting open soil, easing spring,
furrows make neat lines joining
together idle infant Whitewater
and distant whitethorn hedges.
Zulu and Zanzibar speed the plough
to Dalton's words, barely loud enow
to cross the space between them:
the shires' broad shackled backs.

In museums we curate the past
allowing concessions that suit.
Evian in blue moulded polymer,
successor to sweet bottled tea,
swashes to the ploughman's gait
and well-worn Fruits of the Loom
ward off north east winds
sure as any native gansey.

Down Union Drift, Easter's
last tractor trailer ride returns,
signalling the day's last strip.
Slowing beyond the headland
the coulter makes a final cut
turning fields to shining corduroy.
Housman's harness jingles still,
homebound hooves raise clouds.

Edging towards a millennium
we have reached the headland.
From here neat lines arrayed, plots
where pasts are preserved, revered.
Beyond, tomorrow and tomorrow,
the unworked arid earth awaits.
In new times dry dust fogs the air,
motes, fears, bringing tears to eyes.

Gressenhall, 1997

THROUGH AN ENGLISH MIDDLE MARCH

i) Redesdale

Through this last of summer
we follow rivers partnering
the river, remembering those
read of perils of past travellers
and grateful for the shelter
of trees. On heathered moors
about us the purple peace
openly deceives and even here
cold caresses of autumn, the
breezes bringing thistledown,
dart and cross our road:
reconnoitring for old reiver
winter, gathering strength
in some lair beyond the
rolling hills, waiting.

ii) Carter Bar

I cannot tell why we break our journey
on this windblown hill where a tourist
board stack marks what fighting men and
maps know: boundary and border, where
direction or aspiration can make this
strip a beginning or an end. Neither
can I explain my wish to balance
and straddle two lands, twopenny godlike.
Always tardy and unsure with farewells,
perhaps it is fear fixing me to this edge,
or some pride in turning back, seeing
familiar colours as if for the first time.
And into my fascination, a silence we share,
you call to me, from another country now.

iii) Dinner at Otterburn

At the drizzled end of a dull day
with nowhere else to go we follow
deserted roads and snaking tracks
over the lordship of Larriston
to the castle at Hermitage,
looming strong in the forbidding
grisaille of brae and summer scud.
Twentyfive pence buys history enough
to forget for the time of our visit,
a table booked at seven in that land
where the village's fairest daughters
bring salmon to the weary traveller.
So we will be late, they will serve
coy teen smiles for our dilemma and
doubtless I will fluster and hasten
the journey to eat, anxious always
to coincide with the right time. What
I wonder, care these stones for minutes?

TO A ROMAN WALL AUXILIARY
(Vercovicium)

For three weeks the sun shines here:
around wells Brigante girls draw water
and sponge you with sweet as honey smiles
that promise the discovery of secret places
known only to them among folds of moor
and linen. But when cold returns and
tribal doors around the fort are closed,
it is their voices above the roistering
that you hear as you watch and walk each
week of wall, holding the line, keeping
the frontiers men place between each other.

Beyond Kielder's trickling ribbon of burn
cold northerlies mass to head south
like well aimed spears, never failing
to mark and sting with cold their targets,
those bronzed faces guarding parapets.
It is then you know a meaning for loneliness
as you consider possibilities, remote as the wall,
of returning home to a warmer place than this,
where the girl's sighs and ecstacies
ride the howling winds and your loin's dull ache
underlines a being there that knows no belonging.

Yes, you have a status single among family
and friends. You have money and rights
more than mere soil could yield, and the eagle
is benevolent: twenty-five years service and
best prize of all, they make you citizen of Rome.
But never ask the price. Huddle in your hooded cape,
shelter ears against the border's wanton-ness and
a wind that keeps the stench of a garrison low.
Guard an empire, guard against a soldier's solitude,
die if required, but never question causes or conquests
that one day will be just another century's ruins.

A PROSPECT OF DURHAM

Smoke rises from terrace chimneys,
crows circle, fussing over battlements.
through one window, a viaduct,
East coast main line roof rail;
through another, a cathedral,
direct line, Durham to deity.
Lights in the town go off;
in castle great hall, come on.
A single bell tolls.
Someone crosses Palace Green
hunched by cold and cares,
solitary to communion.
The 0715 London King's Cross
takes northern men, the like
of Edmund Byers and Romald Kirk,
through cuttings, south, away south.
Parking cones are marshalled:
a uniformed porter and plastic
against another day's trippers.
Near eight the courtyard echoes: a shot
or the sudden drawing of a bolt.
Doors heave-ho open: day slips in.
River breezes rise now, vapouring breath.
In streets laid out windows away
shopping's earnest business begins.
And from a crenellated hilltop hide,
some other rarified toil drifts down:
this scribbled page, the labour of breathing,
waking words and poor apologies for clouds.

LLANBERIS PASS

Eryri: the domain of eagles.
They circled here once, calls echoing,
watching the devil boiling clouds
in Llyn Llydaw's cauldron
to threaten Caernarfon Bay
and the Menai straitened sailors.
Now RAF rescue rotors hover,
the baser call of another skybird
filling the pass by Glydwr Fawr.

Inland from Llandudno's hotels,
coaches take in castles, crags:
air-conditioned elders overdose
on wonders beyond windows.
We are part of their view,
heady at a gentle height,
by broken bits of mountain,
waving at queues of cars like
slow trailing diecast miniatures.

Arms out-stretched for photos
show sheer size, extent, expanse;
grandparents in another country see
the chasm their offspring conquered.
Arms out-stretched as if to soar
over, beyond Pont-y-Gromlech
through rain that barely is,
ever more like forgotten eagles
as clouds come down to hide us.

JUNE ON SNOW HILL

For GMcK

Snagged on Yr Wyddfa's summit
skies spill cloud over Clogwyn.
Cold air chills the proving somethings
and fog stifles breathless trippers,
blurred by mist and quickly erased.

A sudden break appears,
eddying thermals from Allt Moses,
a small window toward Lake Padarn
'til curtains quickly close again.

Numb and blue in June,
glad of the tearoom's heat,
we huddle and lean bringing life
to tired lungs and chilled limbs.
Outside, mountain ogres clear the cloud,

restoring summer and postcard views.
For the descent we buy iced water,
the hot chocolate urn turned off,
draining now ready for tomorrow.

Note: Snowdon from Old English *snaw dun* meaning snow hill. The Welsh, Yr Wyddfa, shortened from Gwydffa Rhitta (Rhitta's cairn), after the legendary giant Rhitta Gawr who held court in Snowdonia.

SHORE

Shoreline: uncertain edge
where land frays seaward,
wears out or begins again.

Footsteps slowed by sand,
its trickling treachery revealed
when placed under pressure.

Imperceptibly, sly high tides
wash in, tease, sculpt, play,
catch the sun and throw it back,

drift out, deposit debris:
watermarks of weed, flotscum,
discarded razor shells and wrack.

Where water was, a hundred
bubbles betray buried cockles
as if the beach were breathing.

Washed up: a memory, a northern shore,
unfamiliar edge for beginning endings.
An umbrella atop scooped out dunes,

their home's hastily felt-tipped name
on paper handy from her bag,
Chez Nous impaled on marrams

– sea views, open plan, bijou,
no mod cons, closest neighbours
coasters awaiting tides to Blyth –

asserting proud ownership of
the first and only place
built and shared together.

Washed up shore. Unsure line:
waves, detritus, coming, going,
beginnings, endings, ebbing, flowing.

ON A STRATFORD STREET

The day after watching Eccleston's Macbeth
we idle the shared summer by Joules
in the bard's busy trippered High Street.

A distinguished man in cream cottons
comes quipping, teasing tourists with
Don't want the dog... here's a £1 for the lead.

He is embraced by a woman, her hug uneasy
across his shoulders but solace in her words:
Oh Ken. I've just heard. I am so, so sorry....

Their talking over, he walks toward me, pausing
to deliver a tailored jape about bags and labels.
How ill white hairs become a fool and jester,

especially one with rheumy eyes, telling of grief
barely four days new, not sleeping, eating, though
buying newspapers, alone after sixty seven years.

No children to conspire for a Queen's telegram
though one anniversary he had a medal made,
because they said marrying him she deserved one.

For want of words, something to make amends
and shopping having nothing, I offer a hand.
He holds long on it, then off towards Bridge Street

and more random extras to swell a moment or two.
Too late I remember coffee, the '40s tearoom,
but he is gone, alone among crowds and theatres.

There other tragedies are regularly played out,
which despite witty one-liners, without leading ladies
or a strong supporting cast, seldom run for long.

DISCOVERING DAD

On a day clearing your house,
sorting photos from their frames
I find you, much as you probably did
when you cleared your family home,
bringing back the front parlour frame
of you with wartime sergeant's stripes.
Proud, your aircrew melt-hearts smile
almost a pout, you are poised, posed,
your back straight with bearing
and familiar from smaller copies
in the chocolate box of memories.
You must have decided the portrait
too big, dated or dark to display
so ditched, unwanted in a wardrobe.

I prise open rusted clips releasing back
and frame, freeing you from fogged glass.
You and another unfamiliar, unseen you,
the one newly left school in his first job.
Something in the City, insignificant
in cramped offices Mark Lane way.
And with their branches everywhere
Jerome Studio's catch a Forest Gate boy
reflective at fifteen, a smirk for a smile.
The lean, drab thirties hang from him:
wide crumpled lapels, a cobbled collar
distinctly more raffish than RAF
and wearing the insouciant look
of a James Dean before his time.

Was my grandmother too poor or frugal
to buy another frame, leaving her son
forgotten, behind his serviceman self?
Did you ever know what she did,
maybe wonder what became of
the one photo showing you carefree?
If I did not believe you did not know
you were there, lost in time's palimpsest,
I would think you had planned this.
One last surprise, one last meeting
in the cold, emptied lounge you left;
to see you, once, just like me, yet with
no opportunity to talk or ask questions,
quite the way you always preferred.

AND WHAT OF PLOUGHMEN?

Let us remember pasts, journeys
when speeds were fixed at fifty
and student subs stretched to
express coaches between towns,
where beds were cold or shared.
Pitsford, Brixworth, Lamport Hall:
there was history enough passing
through shires where sheep grazed
and lambs frisked fields marked
by medieval ploughs and furrows.

Then destinations, aching partings
in dieseled municipal bus stations
all thirties kitsch, brick and steel,
built where lead works once were.
Lovers care little for built styles
meeting buses in, waving buses out
through a long summer of smiles
giving way to tears – heavy hearts
from lead in the air or endings.
And those who loved, stayed or left

where, how did history leave them?
Separated now by miles: long routes
where scheduled services are rare.
Consumed by the changing years,
time and transport no longer connect
moments shared, broken by distance.
And forsaking furlongs for village girls
did ploughmen scarring earth with strips
and sweat, with love and baser needs
touch hearts for years, or barely months?

NIGHT NOISES

Purposeful parcel trains, fussy goods,
far off factories shifting towards dawn,
churches, town hall towers tolling time:

night muffled city sounds reassuring
in those silent and unsleeping hours
when hearts first held uneasy sway.

Years on heard again, far from family:
the desperate insomnia of separation,
the same single university beds.

Narrow enough for one, but two...
as well they didn't care (though did,
at first) feeding on the intimacy

of not sleeping, falling out of bed,
before the slow falling out of love,
neither able to hold the other in.

Familiar sounds return. Less shunting,
fewer factories, but night noises still,
haunting loud with folly and regret.

LOOKING AT REMAINS

i)
We celebrate historical remains differently.
Romans left us roads, walls and stones,
seldom-random earthworks, like scars,
which we mark alongside, with tarmac parks
for coaches, cars & coffee vans (Easter-Oct).

ii)
At the roadside lime kiln lack of space
dictates merely a National Park board.
It speaks of a more recent past
when kilns burned limestone,
calcined lime for soil or mortar.
It alone remains, of hundreds.

iii)
Before their day began dying,
bleeding into Cumberland,
it was here they paused
to dull the ache of walking,
light headed from dehydrating,
when plastic-bottled water
was still to be invented.

iv)
There were no interpretive panels,
the Park an unsophisticated place then,
just two brick-lined caves in the bank.
And if there had been would they have told
the distance to a village anywhere,
the nearest public hide-and-speak,
or times for the last train home,
Bardon Mill-Newcastle [SO-Sundays only]?

v)
They had walked the wall,
talked the talk of lovers,
taken sandwiches in Tupperware
and hard boiled eggs in shells.

Where Asturian auxiliaries shivered
and regiments of ramblers shambled,
they stopped, spread-out their parkas
and overlooking Crag Lough's waters,
snuggled too long in each other's arms,
when how far to go hardly mattered.

vi)
And then the ceaseless moorland,
mile after mile of die-straight roads,
stock-free coarse-grassed fields,
the rolling heathered hills, bothies,
glimpses of distant unreachable farms:
the weight of anxiety, twenty years new,
far from familiars and home, like a Roman.

vii)
A mile or so from where they waited,
down the Stanegate a year or so before,
at Vindolanda, were unearthed letters:
handwritten, gum arabic and water
on thin tablets of oak, birch or alder,
their words soon lost from oxidising.

Not so her letters: their secrets
shoe-boxed, dusty and undisturbed,
blue Parker Quink and Queen's Velvet
reminding when three and a half pence
bought first class with two deliveries daily
and often there was something in each.

viii)
Health Warning: love, like lime,
burns and is an irritant to eyes.

ix)
In a recent unrelated procedure
the surgeon was able to confirm
no evidence of cardiac scarring
attributable to events back then,
although at the time it felt so.

x)
Four decades later he passes here,
stops to read an interpretive board.
Crindledykes kilns they're called.
Not that it would have helped lost souls
but good the remains have a name,
hard as the landscapes they walked.

xi)
It is reassuring to mark histories.
As memory fades it is a steep uphill
remembering things seen, discovered:
how downsoft hidden skin could feel,
the gentle teasings of first time lips
and the giddy sweetness of a kiss.

DRYTIME TRAVELLER

At sunset the umbrella'd fishing men
grown single by the water's edge,
close slowly for night. Tomorrow
when I take again this road to your bed
and sit with gods and saints others have
invoked to hold you here, they will
be blossoming brighter, fresher, hopeful.
So I will come to keep you from dying.

In these empty lands I know of no
means to measure my dread of death.
At Stonea occasional trains cross the fen
shimmering in the haze of miles away.
Few trees to measure speed, only the shade
midway of a gatekeeper's hut, hurtled by –
but from here, a slow, imperceptible
progress between unseen stations.

Here they have rubbed away the line
between field and sky: no boundaries,
no distinctions. Earth and heaven blur,
become one beyond the low grumble of pumps
diverting water to dried and distant fields.
There man-made rain mists round and round,
at times catching up the sun. These days,
these places, we make our own rainbows:
there is perhaps hope in that.

Understanding no rites but those of the earth,
knowing no faith save the certainty that men
in dry times will ease the season's passage,
my relics are roots bared, withering
before the sun, crying scorched for a rainbow.
Travelling through days marred by melancholy,
without bread or wine, hope is simple things:
like sharing the taste of strawberries,
first ever of hoped for summers to come.

NOTES ON RETURNING

For Geraldeen

Back now to the old way, those
remembered places and patterns you
knew and once helped give meaning to.

Friends find it easier to talk and,
pouring tea, wear faces of relief,
less afraid now to disturb our grief.

Days arrive separate, seem less blurred,
with time for duties left, or to recall
words spoken then that went unheard.

And sorting through the life you left
boxes are graveyards of memories sharp
as moments you saved these things to mark.

Doctors call less now that you are gone
and you would smile to see us reworking
well worn moulds of familiar ways retrieved

from distant days, more special now
for those whose hands you squeezed,
who kissed your lips before cold set in.

PAPWORTH POEMS

i) Some women enter your heart...

A first lost love once lamented
unlike others, her heart did more
than pump blood around a body.
Jolted thus, he coasted through years
of love and loss, thinking it could be said,
that, short of wearing them on a sleeve,

for a man, he did his emotions well.
Then hearts enlarged with signs of wear,
believing he'd loved wisely, if too much.
When another finds her way, enters his heart
and probes, explores with science and data.
She smiles, mouths sweet-sounding numbers

suggesting – cruel irony – it was not love
or longing making hearts full to breaking,
but syndromes which, cured, could cause it
shrink and settle back, despite the bag
it came in being lost. Remodelling,
she said, as though they talked of clay.

So for the muscle's sake, think downsizing:
wonder which feelings or emotions are kept,
which urgings to throw or longings discard,
sorting a lifetime caught, trapped in a pump.
But by the end it stays the same, no change:
just better ordered, stacked and understood.

ii) Veering

There are lines, some in sand, to tread,
others, undrawn, along tiled corridors
which, completed straight and true,
herald discharge from a hospital bed.

The grand finale a flight of stairs,
the clipboard boxes almost ticked,
fully defrosted, capacities restored,
when someone says, "See, he veers."

With trajectory broken, disconnected,
no option but stay another day.
The ward's plastic chairs revisited,
menu choices waiting to be selected.

Night brings time to ponder aiming straight.
Hard after a lifetime easily deflected,
wide of the mark and aimlessly drifting,
to plot a course, steer and never deviate.

Another collection by Paul Berry from Troubador is described overleaf

TOWARDS BABINGLEY

ISBN: 978 1803137 049

In this collection, Paul Berry continues to be inspired by landscape, often drawing on his Norfolk heritage. Other poems highlight a growing reputation as a chronicler of love, loss and longing. The strength of his writing, whether portraying people, the lives they lead or spaces they inhabit, is to reflect and celebrate the extraordinary nature of the ordinary and everyday.

Towards Babingley is a space where life experiences are explored from a wellspring of the poet's connection with nature. His ability to combine words to create vibrant images are a hallmark of his poetry and the reader will find themselves enriched by his perceptions and philosophical hints. It is a many layered approach, giving his poems a link with the past and also a glimpse of the future.
Margi Blunden

Paul Berry takes us on a poetical tour, a dizzying ride extending out from Babingley to the Midlands, Yorkshire, Wales, the Lake District and the North East, taking in many aspects and experiences of lives lived in the last few decades or so. Garlanded throughout with superb nature writing and enduring images, this book will appeal to anyone living through a period of great change.
Martin Chown

The ability to transport the reader is a very real skill which Berry has, drawing them out of themselves in a most gentle way. He questions the meaning of deep relationships, experienced many years ago, in lines of beautiful, rhythmically coherent words... (whose) sound becomes deeply evocative and meaningful – lines which will chime with many people's experiences.
Peter Coates

Past finalist in the Eric Gregory Awards
PAUL BERRY

Towards Babingley

a poetry collection

This book is printed on paper from sustainable sources managed under the Forest Stewardship Council (FSC) scheme.

It has been printed in the UK to reduce transportation miles and their impact upon the environment.

For every new title that Troubador publishes, we plant a tree to offset CO_2, partnering with the More Trees scheme.

For more about how Troubador offsets its environmental impact, see www.troubador.co.uk/sustainability-and-community